HOW GOD MOVED MY ASHTRAY

A Devotional Experience

John "Little John" Paladino

Foreword by Matthew Maher,
Speaker & Author of U MAY B THE ONLY BIBLE SOMEBODY READS

Cover Design: Propel Marketing, LLC
Editing: Joanna Sanders LLC
Layout & Formatting: Joanna Sanders LLC

To Matt:

Words can hardly express the gratitude I feel in my heart for having met you. It is because of your outward expression of love for Jesus and your unwavering example to me, that I am now saved.

God's light through you, is what led me to Christ, even in the darkness. Thank you, my friend, for caring enough to show me this newfound faith that has saved my life.

I love you and cherish our friendship very much. My friendship and loyalty are yours for life.

John "Little John" Paladino

Servus Servorum Dei

Contents

FOREWORD

I've heard it said that experience is the best teacher! And though this proverb may hold valuable truth, it is often the heavy experiences, those wrapped in pain and suffering, that force us to count the cost and truly appreciate the price paid for our souls.

I've had the privilege of witnessing first-hand, the transformation of this man's big heart. And not only because of all the hard experiences in his life, but for the exacting cost of pain that became the necessary dynamic to lead John "Little John" Paladino to Christ. A cost that was paid in full at Calvary's cross; as there is nothing else that could wash a man clean from shame, guilt, and pain—but the blood of Christ.

This devotional is not just his personal record of how he took the appropriate baby steps towards real faith in Christ at the cross. Rather, it was his sincere devotion to the experience, moved by the power of the Holy Spirit, that birthed the desire within him to share his surrendered journey in the hopes that others may follow suit.

John's willingness to be so pointed and transparent will allow you to travel the same path that brought a bold, feisty and unsettled former gangster into a humbled, peaceful and surrendered man of God. You will hear how his faith was tested and how he had to relearn "new things" and put away "old behaviors." John's honest approach invites you to come alongside of him in this journey, providing helpful insights in learning the disciplines of what it takes to step into a surrendered life.

I am beyond grateful that I was not only a witness to his experience, but that John himself has honored me by calling me his "Accountability Shepherd." I am humbled to be the one that God entrusted to lead "Little John" to the water of the Word by making him curiously thirsty. And to God be all the glory, it is only the water of the Word (the Holy Spirit) that can quench an empty man's thirst when he is willing and open to such outpouring.

Since Memorial Day 2011, I have watched John grow in his faith as he lives up to the steps he outlines in this devotional. And as all who were at Mid-State Prison with us can attest, this big giant of a man bore his soul to anyone who was willing to listen, as he always began his conversation, "*You wanna hear how God moved my ashtray?*"

I am so proud of "Little John" and I know God will use him and this devotional as it is a Christ-centered expression of his heart. Please continue to be in prayer for John for the mighty ways that this man of God is positioned to be used.

Imprisoned by peace,

Matthew Maher
Former Professional Soccer Player
President, Soldiers For Faith Ministries
Teaching Pastor, Coastal Christian Ocean City, NJ
Author of: *U May B the Only Bible Somebody Reads, Imprisoned by Peace, & Unchained.*

www.TruthOverTrend.com

INTRODUCTION

From an early age, my life was devoted to chaos and destruction. I began to hone my craft at just twelve years old, stealing, robbing, cheating, and committing serious crimes. I was, as Paul references in the Bible, "the chief of sinners." I am an unlikely case for having found the truth of joy in Christ and it is only by God's grace alone that I live in His peace now, at the age of 46.

But before Christ came into my life, my life of crime came with a high cost; including years in institutions and correctional facilities. I have done time in most of the prisons in the state of New Jersey, two Federal Penitentiaries, several county jails, and two half-way houses. I've had what seemed like countless years on probation and parole. Throughout even extensive correction, my motive for most of the crimes I committed remained the cold hard cash associated with the payoff.

And while the suffering was significant, I never once blamed anyone else for any of the confinements that I've had to endure. I played and I paid.

Miraculously enough I've also survived several car wrecks, one of which landed my blazer under an 18-wheeler, killing my passenger; a childhood friend named Matt. Another time, I crashed my motorcycle at 60 mph into a parked limousine while wearing nothing but shorts and a pair of boots. I was thrown about 20 feet into the air and my leg was crushed when I landed nearly 50 feet away. I walk with a limp to this day. I cannot explain my survival of a life like this without acknowledging that God must still have use for me.

I used to pridefully think I had beaten the grim reaper out of my life having survived these among other poorly chosen situations. If I had been a cat, I would have rationalized that I had about two or three lives left. But since God has opened my eyes, I now realize that I have only one life; the most important of all – that of eternal life.

I am now a believer and have accepted Jesus as my personal Lord and Savior. I have an abiding and growing faith in God and can testify through my experience and first-hand knowledge that He is always listening.

Memorial Day 2011 was the day I became reborn as a Christian. These are the steps that led me from that moment, into a life of submission and blessed peace, found in Him alone.

John "Little John" Paladino

I WOULD HAVE LOST HEART, UNLESS I HAD BELIEVED THAT I WOULD SEE THE GOODNESS OF THE LORD IN THE LAND OF THE LIVING.

PSALM 27:13

SAUL TO PAUL

THE LORD IS NOT SLACK CONCERNING HIS PROMISE, AS SOME COUNT SLACKNESS, BUT IS LONGSUFFERING TOWARD US, NOT WILLING THAT ANY SHOULD PERISH BUT THAT ALL SHOULD COME TO REPENTANCE.

2 PETER 3:9

It all began one evening in May 2011, the night before Memorial Day, during my fourth stint to prison. I made a facetious request of sorts to God. Another inmate and myself were talking about God and while I admitted a need for change in my life, I was vocal to confirm my doubt that it would ever happen. My reasons were solid and lined up. First, I had worked hard to establish a reputation as a "tough guy" and was not interested in giving that up, and second, I admitted that I wasn't really convinced about God anyway. To me, the men who had miraculously "found God" in prison seemed weak and desperate.

As Vinney and I debated back and forth, I said, "Wouldn't it be so much easier if we could just ask God to move this ashtray across the table? And then, I would definitely believe in Him." We talked through the night; the ashtray only moving when Vinney moved it himself, to put ashes in it or to extinguish his cigarette.

With heavy eyes, I went to bed thinking nothing more of my bravado suggestion to God. At that moment, I didn't know or understand that He could see exactly what was going on in my heart. He knew that deep down (in a place that I didn't want to show anyone else), I really desired change, peace, and to be saved by something. He knew I was searching. I seriously wanted God to move that ashtray.

The next day, Memorial Day 2011, I was asked to read some passages from a Daily Bread booklet for a fellowship group I was attending. My fellow inmate and friend Matt Maher, was the leader of our group. I had been attending this Bible group, not because I was a Christian, but because of him. I respected Matt and wanted to support him in his ministry, and so I sat there daily, listening to his teaching. I must admit I found it interesting and at times, it stirred my heart.

I confidently picked up the Daily Bread as asked, to begin reading the passages. As I attempted to read, something suddenly and unexpectedly overwhelmed my spirit. I could see the words but only two or three of them came out of my mouth. I was breaking down in tears for no good reason in a way that felt completely outside of my control. It was surreal. I had no idea what was happening. I tried again desperately to read the Word and regain my composure. The whole ordeal of showing emotional vulnerability was unfamiliar territory to me. I couldn't remember the last time I cried. And publicly? Me? Never!

With all eyes on me, I got up looking confused and out of sorts. I could see the other inmates shocked and amazed looks, trying to figure out what was going on, mouths wide open. They were just as confused as I was watching me struggle to maintain my composure. No one uttered a word. They couldn't fathom this 300 lb. "tough guy" breaking down by simply attempting to read the Word of God. I excused myself momentarily and headed quickly to the bathroom. Splashing water on my face, I tried my best to wash away the feelings that were flooding out of me. I spoke to myself in the mirror, "Come on John! What are you doing? Pull yourself together, you're a tough guy, a gangster. Don't cry in front of these guys, don't let your interior be exposed, don't let your armor be dented or stripped, stand strong!"

I gathered myself together- or so I thought- and went back to the group. I tried to joke it off by saying it was something I ate, but as I once again picked up the booklet and tried to read the words, nothing came out of my mouth but gut-wrenching sobs.

There I sat, a hardened and notorious mobster, crying openly in front of the entire tier, choking out muffled words in between sobs. *What in the world was happening to me?*

Deep down I knew I wanted peace in my heart like I had witnessed from Matt and another Pastor that had recently visited the prison. I explained to the group, how I went to church with Matt the night before, and listened to the speaker give his testimony and my heart was stirred. I could no longer deny what I had observed in these men living their lives with such confounding peace, confidence and fortitude that I had never seen. I confessed that I wanted what these men had, and I realized God was sending me a clear message at that very moment that I could have it because He was listening to my heart's yearnings all along. I declared that I wanted to ask Jesus to be my personal Savior.

I got through the fellowship group and felt cleansed and peaceful. My day went on as usual but I felt consumed with the perplexing thoughts of trying to understand what had happened. The day's events were weighing on my mind.

That night I went to bed and just as I was dozing off to sleep, it hit me ever so clearly. I sprung up and called to Matt, (his bunk is next to mine) and said, "Bro, that was God moving my ashtray!"

You see, my challenge to God to move an ashtray was such a foolish and miniscule task that any magician could have accomplished it. It occurred to me that God was showing- not only to me- but to all those present that night, that He could do a much greater work than move a simple ashtray. He could move a tough guy's very hard heart.

That night I got the best sleep I've had in years.

This was the undeniable day that God moved me from Saul to Paul. I once was just like Saul, a persecutor of Christians. I had my own beliefs, which to me, meant that everyone else was wrong. I found weakness where they found strength. I saw conformity as a deficiency when I was an outlaw. I watched them gather in peace and harmony, while I walked alone in total chaos and destruction. While Christians sang, prayed, and praised, I thought of others' demise, and condemned as many as I could.

The Saul in me thought this was how I should act, how I should think. I found no fault in my own eyes. I believed I exemplified power, strength, and my own form of righteousness, that is, until I met Christ. I didn't meet Him on the road to Damascus, but on an empty dead-end road in prison; where I sat for years at a time without seeing a way out.

My eyes were blind until the day I met Christ. He opened them and now I see more clearly than I've ever seen before. Christ touched my heart and gave me a new name deep in my soul. I went from Saul to Paul and am now a new man. I now see strength in my weakness. I now sing and praise. I now pray in peace. I now uplift and encourage. I now conform and speak softly. I now have faith in Christ with all things. I now, am Paul.

And so in this day, I want to encourage you that no matter where you are, God can bring you to a new life. He can give you a new name. He can make you a new man or woman. There is no where you have been that

He hasn't already accounted for and redeemed by the blood of His Son, Jesus Christ.

God's promise to us is if we believe in Him and accept His Son Jesus the Christ as our personal Savior, then He has a place for us in Heaven. God's very own sacrifice of His Son shows us just how much He loves us and the lengths He is willing to go, to save us from the fiery pit of hell.

Your own redemption is just a prayer away.

While accepting Jesus Christ as your personal Savior is the first step to your new life, I realize that you may not be ready to do so. Believe me, I understand where you are at, and I encourage you to keep reading through this devotional to allow me to share what I have learned. You may come back to this part at any time. But when your heart moves, and when you hear the sound of His voice in it (Hebrews 3:15), I urge you not to wait any longer.

Accepting Jesus as Your Personal Savior

FOR GOD SO LOVED THE WORLD THAT HE GAVE HIS ONLY BEGOTTEN SON, THAT WHOEVER BELIEVES IN HIM SHOULD NOT PERISH BUT HAVE EVERLASTING LIFE.
JOHN 3:16

Jesus went willingly to His death on the cross in order to save us from eternal punishment for our sinful ways. His spilled blood can cleanse the worst of sinners. When we know this truth, how can we not ask Him to enter our hearts and to save us from our own sinful nature and carnal flesh? How could we not have enough faith in Him to ask for His mercy and forgiveness? With a heartfelt, personal acknowledgement, we can be cleansed and forgiven of all our wrongs. The Bible says, "if we confess with our mouth that Jesus is Lord and believe in our heart that God has raised Him from the dead, that we will be saved" (Romans 10:9). How much easier could God have made it for us to join Him in the Glories of Heaven?

For me it was as simple as asking Jesus to forgive me for my sins and to come into my life as my personal Savior. I asked that in a simple prayer and finished with the statement that I submit my life and my will to God and Jesus with the utmost faith.

Two simple sentences privately spoken to God in a prayer, paved the way to my rebirth as a Christian; with a clean slate and a new beginning.

Pray and ask Jesus to enter your heart and soul, acknowledge that God raised Him from the dead, humbly ask Him to forgive you of your past, present and future sins and invite Jesus to come into your life as your personal Savior. Your redemption is as easy as that! Today is a great day, for your rebirth.

AND HE SAID TO ME. "MY GRACE IS SUFFICIENT FOR YOU, FOR MY STRENGTH IS MADE PERFECT IN WEAKNESS." THEREFORE, MOST GLADLY, I WILL RATHER BOAST IN MY INFIRMITIES THAT THE POWER OF CHRIST MAY REST UPON ME.

2 CORINTHIANS 12:9

EVEN WHEN WE WERE DEAD IN TRESPASSES, MADE US ALIVE TOGETHER WITH CHRIST (BY GRACE YOU HAVE BEEN SAVED), AND RAISED US UP TOGETHER, AND MADE US SIT TOGETHER IN THE HEAVENLY PLACES IN CHRIST JESUS, THAT IN THE AGES TO COME HE MIGHT SHOW THE EXCEEDING RICHES OF HIS GRACE IN HIS KINDNESS TOWARD US IN CHRIST JESUS.

EPHESIANS 2:5-7

DO NOT REMEMBER THE FORMER THINGS, NOR CONSIDER THE THINGS OF OLD. BEHOLD, I WILL DO A NEW THING, NOW IT SHALL SPRING FORTH; SHALL YOU NOT KNOW IT? I WILL EVEN MAKE A ROAD IN THE WILDERNESS AND RIVERS IN THE DESERT. THE BEAST OF THE FIELD WILL HONOR ME, THE JACKALS AND THE OSTRICHES, BECAUSE I GIVE WATERS IN THE WILDERNESS AND RIVERS IN THE DESERT, TO GIVE DRINK TO MY PEOPLE, MY CHOSEN. THIS PEOPLE I HAVE FORMED FOR MYSELF; THEY SHALL DECLARE MY PRAISE.

ISAIAH 43:18-21

YOU ARE FORGIVEN!

IF WE CONFESS OUR SINS, HE IS FAITHFUL AND JUST TO FORGIVE US OUR SINS AND TO CLEANSE US FROM ALL UNRIGHTEOUSNESS.

1 JOHN 1:9

Over the months since God "moved my ashtray" and I accepted Jesus Christ as my personal Savior, I have often wondered about sin, especially my own past sins. I wondered how I could erase them or be unburdened from the many horrific things attached to my previous life of crime.

I knew the answer was that I had been released from them because of God's divine intervention through Jesus, and I knew that I had received that gift. But I still couldn't fully grasp that *all* of my sins had been washed clean and reconciled by God. I kept worrying about my past wrong doings. I needed to learn how to rely on God to remind me that all my past sins were wiped clean, fully paid for, and settled once and for all.

I remind myself daily that I was forgiven the moment I repented and asked God to forgive me for all those sins that plagued my heart. I prayed and told God what He knew already of the depth and darkness of my sin. I pleaded, "Please God forgive me and help me to be a stronger man, one who is able to fight my fleshy desires and worldly temptations." I realized that my attempt to condemn myself for my past was also an ungodly temptation.

When I asked Jesus to come into my heart, soul, and life as my personal Savior, He did so unconditionally. The blood He shed on the cross for my sins has cleansed me of all of my past, present, and future sins (And can for yours as well).

I am finally getting that I simply don't need to try to retain "guilt" for the sins He's already paid the price for. If I have confessed them, truly repented and requested God's forgiveness, then I can be settled, that they are settled.

God does not want us beating ourselves up over our past. He has washed our slate clean. If we are now reborn by the blood of Christ; in His mercy, and by

Jesus' all-atoning sacrifice, God has forgiven us. God wants His goodness, not Satan's guilt, to fill us. All we have to do is believe in His Son as our Savior, be filled with His Holy Spirit, and our past transgressions will be wiped away.

He wants us to resist future temptation to sin. And when we do fall, He desires for us to "confess our sins and He will forgive us and cleanse us from all unrighteousness" (1 John 1:9).

Do you believe today that you can be completely and totally forgiven? Forgiveness is God's mercy upon and available for us all.

... TO OPEN THEIR EYES, IN ORDER TO TURN THEM FROM DARKNESS TO LIGHT, AND FROM THE POWER OF SATAN TO GOD, THAT THEY MAY RECEIVE FORGIVENESS OF SINS AND AN INHERITANCE AMONG THOSE WHO ARE SANCTIFIED BY FAITH IN ME.

ACTS 26:18

REPENT THEREFORE AND BE CONVERTED, THAT YOUR SINS MAY BE BLOTTED OUT, SO THAT TIMES OF REFRESHING MAY COME FROM THE PRESENCE OF THE LORD...

ACTS 3:9

BLIND FAITH

NOW FAITH IS THE SUBSTANCE OF THINGS HOPED FOR, THE EVIDENCE OF THINGS NOT SEEN.
HEBREWS 11:1

You may still have a hard time understanding how I could go from a life of condemning Christian believers to having faith in a God that I could not "see." This "blind faith" of sorts is actually not all that unusual in our experience. We deal with blind faith every day in our lives.

Most people go to work 40 hours a week and anticipate getting paid at the end of that week, or even the end of the next. Blind faith that your employer will pay you.

Ever jump from a plane at 30,000 feet? Blind faith that the parachute will open.

An elevator ride to the top floor. Blind faith that the cables will hold.

A flight to a vacation destination, a ride on a cruise ship, a roller coaster, or the daily commute over the bridge or through the tunnel—all blind faith!

So why is it so hard for us to believe in a merciful God that exists beyond our limited "sight?" Although we can't see God, we can feel Him through the miracles He performs in our lives and around us daily. We have often heard it compared to not being able to see the wind, but we are assured of it as it blows by our face or moves the trees around us. My point is that blind faith isn't as unusual as we make it out to be. We were wired to operate in many areas of our life by this very principle - trusting in the unseen.

If we open our eyes to God's message, our faith doesn't have to be blind. He's opened the eyes of the "blind" on many recorded occasions. We can ask Him for "eyes that can see" and we may receive vision to understand Him in ways which surely may still seem like "blind faith" to others. He is everywhere; some just don't see His hand in creation. I may not see Him physically, but I believe because I can feel Him and see Him move in my life. I can see His works and read His word. I blindly walk through life putting faith in man's creations and operations, so why wouldn't I "blindly" have faith in my God, the God who created it *all*!

FOR WE WALK BY FAITH, NOT BY SIGHT.

2 CORINTHIANS 5:7

START PRAYING

For You, Lord, are good, and ready to forgive, and abundant in mercy to all those who call upon You. Give ear, O Lord, to my prayer; and attend to the voice of my supplications. In the day of my trouble I will call upon You, For You will answer me.
Psalm 86:5-7

It's funny to me how some people idly pray - supposedly to God - even though they have never accepted Jesus Christ as their personal Savior and therefore have no relationship with God. I recognize the contrast in this now since I used to do exactly that.

Some people pray while they're hugging "the porcelain throne" after a hard night of drinking. "Oh God, please

God, I'll never drink again," repeated a hundred times as they wretch their insides out. Or the whispered one-liners when they want something significant, "Oh Jesus, give me the win, the break, the promotion" etc.

My personal favorite has been my very own prayer while lying in my prison cell on a hard bunk in my confined space, prior to knowing Jesus as my Savior. I would feel what I thought were "evil spirits" waking me from my sleep and I would be paralyzed with fear not wanting to open my eyes dreading something evil in front of me.

So, I would start to pray to God, a God at the time, that I had no faith in, or any relationship with, but I would still utter His name praying and asking for help and protection from this "evil spirit."

The feeling of evil in that cell with me would be so overpowering and have me so scared, and yet when morning came, I'd forget about any conversation with God and go right back to being a godless sinner. The chief of sinners amongst men.

When we utter desperate prayers to God, with no interest of truly knowing Him as our Savior, nor believing in Him wholeheartedly with unwavering faith, then we may as well be yelling a stranger's name out in a crowd. They may turn, but won't recognize who is calling.

Faith based prayer, as I have come to find out, is one of the strongest tools and weapons we have. God has provided this personal means for us to speak with Him one-on-one and the act of prayer guards and protects us against the devil who "roams around like a roaring lion seeking someone to devour" (1 Peter 5:8).

Prayer has helped me so much with my Christian walk. It has allowed me to submit to God's will and ask Him on a personal level to work in my life, give me direction, strength, and understanding in His word and His ways.

A simple prayer thanking God for another day or praising Him for the good works He has performed in your life, means a lot to Him; just as much as a simple "thank you" might mean to you.

God says we don't have to be in church to pray to Him nor do we have to be on bended knee, all we have to do is talk to Him like we would a dear friend, a father, or mentor. He is listening to us always.

Although our prayers may not be answered exactly how we ask them to be answered, God in His infinite wisdom will give us what we need, not what we want.

My advice to all who will listen is to pray daily, pray often. Ask God to help with your problems. Form a relationship with Him and ask God to direct you through trials and tribulations. Express your gratitude and praise Him for your life.

Prayer is strength!

BE ANXIOUS FOR NOTHING, BUT IN EVERYTHING BY PRAYER AND SUPPLICATION, WITH THANKSGIVING, LET YOUR REQUESTS BE MADE KNOWN TO GOD...

PHILIPPIANS 4:6

THEN HE SAID TO ME, "DO NOT FEAR, DANIEL, FOR FROM THE FIRST DAY THAT YOU SET YOUR HEART TO UNDERSTAND, AND TO HUMBLE YOURSELF BEFORE YOUR GOD, YOUR WORDS WERE HEARD AND I HAVE COME BECAUSE OF YOUR WORDS.

DANIEL 10:12

PRAY WITHOUT CEASING.

1THESSALONIANS 5:17

PICK UP A BIBLE

HOW CAN A YOUNG MAN CLEANSE HIS WAY? BY TAKING HEED ACCORDING TO YOUR WORD.
PSALM 119:9

Since becoming a Christian, I've found strength and beauty in God's Word through daily reading from the Bible, and by using *The Daily Bread*, *The Daily Light*, and other devotionals to get in touch with Him and what He is saying to me.

Sometimes after a prayer asking for God's direction on something, I will "randomly" pick a verse or two, to study from the Bible. It is amazing how often I find the wisdom, knowledge and mercy needed to understand my present situation, directly in His Word.

When I start the day off by reading God's precious Word, it guarantees my day will begin on a positive note. It is also a reminder that I must walk a certain way as a Christian. God's way always paves the path in spite of my good intentions. He is faithful to guide me.

Throughout the day, I find myself reading my Bible or other Christian based material for knowledge, reference or to see how God wants me to act. Every day is a learning experience and God's Word shows me how to live.

At night before I go to bed, a quick verse or two sets the tone for my nightly prayers and assists me in having a peaceful night's rest. By closing my day with God's Word, it enables me to process the daily trials and tribulations with a clearer view.

God's Word is just one more way He uses to speak to us. Some of it is like reading a letter from those we love: our fathers, mothers, brothers, sisters, or friends. God uses His Word to reach His people and since His Word is alive and active (Hebrews 4:12), it speaks to all of us in different ways. All we have to do is pick up the Bible, open it, and start to read. It's that simple.

> DRAW NEAR TO GOD AND HE WILL DRAW NEAR TO YOU. CLEANSE YOUR HANDS, YOU SINNERS; AND PURIFY YOUR

HEARTS, YOU DOUBLE-MINDED.

JAMES 4:8

ALL SCRIPTURE IS GIVEN BY INSPIRATION OF GOD, AND IS PROFITABLE FOR DOCTRINE, FOR REPROOF, FOR CORRECTION, FOR INSTRUCTION IN RIGHTEOUSNESS, THAT THE MAN OF GOD MAY BE COMPLETE, THOROUGHLY EQUIPPED FOR EVERY GOOD WORK.

2 TIMOTHY 3:16

FIND A CHURCH OR FELLOWSHIP GROUP

FOR WHERE TWO OR THREE ARE GATHERED TOGETHER IN MY NAME, I AM THERE IN THE MIDST OF THEM.
MATTHEW 18:20

Three months before I accepted Jesus Christ as my personal Savior, I sat with my "accountability shepherd" and brother-in-Christ, Matt Maher.

Upon arriving in this prison, I was placed on Unit Seven East, where Matt had just been moved a few days earlier, from another unit where he spent 14 months. We were placed on the same tier with our bunks right beside one another.

We were an unlikely duo: he, a young man, who made one fatal mistake; and me, the seasoned convict. Our friendship was the model version of a prison odd couple. Matt, who was raised in a Christian home and declared Christ as his Savior from a young age, did what lifelong Christians do; he spoke to me about God.

God in his infinite wisdom gave me the patience and ears to listen and hear all that Matt had to say about being and becoming a Christian saved by the blood of Christ.

On this one particular day as Matt and I were talking, he mentioned how he had started a fellowship group on the unit he had come from and wanted to do the same up here on this unit.

In prison, religion has a stigma of not being cool. Many believe that only the weak go to church to find God. I agreed to sit in to show some support for him. Being the rebellious and notorious gangster that I was, I knew my presence would speak loudly.

In the beginning, I showed up just to support him and figured others would come if they saw me attend. But I also felt compelled to do so because there was something different about him. I liked him as a person.

I also enjoyed hearing Matt tell these interesting stories. He had such a vast variety that he enthusiastically told every day; little anecdotes, some funny, others paraphrased straight from the Scriptures. They helped me gain Biblical knowledge.

I became more attentive to God's Word and started to read and regularly ask questions. Eventually, I even had the opportunity to run some of the fellowship groups in Matt's absence. I told a few of my own anecdotes, some funny, some knowledgeable, and strangely enough, even gave out some stern warnings to accept Christ as Savior (which I had not yet done at this point). I know now that being around the Word each day, was the beginning of Christ knocking on the door of my hard heart.

I always spoke God's Word loudly so all could hear. In retrospect, I see that I had a desire for my voice to carry through the air and give rise to someone (like me) who needed God in their lives. I was feeling His nudge.

Aside from the fellowship group, Matt and I attended church in the prison gym every Sunday night. Every week a different speaker came in to preach a sermon on the cost of sin, righteousness, and how God changed their lives. They all had their own personalities. Some of them would yell their sermons and dance around a little. The ones I liked the most were the guys who used their lives as an example to show that they had been in my shoes, had a drink or two, chased women and led a sinful life. And that somehow, some way, Christ found His way into their lives. It was because of the witness of one such pastor, along with Matt, that I decided to accept the Lord Jesus as my personal Savior.

So, every day at 10:30am, the unit became my church during our fellowship group. Every Sunday night the prison gym became my church, sitting there next to weights and machines on the basketball court. I am still in awe that it was there in a dingy makeshift room, that I listened to men and women preach God's Word. I considered that "church," my church. How beautiful is that?

Matt shared with me the verse that is listed at the beginning of this chapter, from Matthew 18:20. It was then that I realized that even though we were locked up away from the world, we had the opportunity to hold church anywhere that two or three men gathered.

We as Christians all together make God's church. It is not a building, but a body of believers with a common goal of getting to know Christ in a more personal way. He doesn't care where we meet—whether in a gym, an all-purpose room, or right by our bunks. He is there in our midst.

And I've found that it is with like-minded people in the faith that allows and supports each person to grow in a stronger commitment of their own faith while collaboratively building a community of believers. It is a necessity for our growth.

I would highly suggest to find some like-minded believers where God has planted you, and watch something amazing grow.

AND LET US CONSIDER ONE ANOTHER IN ORDER TO STIR UP LOVE AND GOOD WORKS, NOT FORSAKING THE ASSEMBLING OF OURSELVES TOGETHER, AS IS THE MANNER OF SOME, BUT EXHORTING ONE ANOTHER, AND SO MUCH THE MORE AS YOU SEE THE DAY APPROACHING.

HEBREWS 10:24-25

FIND A CHRISTIAN ACCOUNTABILITY SHEPHERD

AS IRON SHARPENS IRON, SO A MAN SHARPENS THE COUNTENANCE OF HIS FRIEND.
PROVERBS 27:17

One of the ways to grow in the Lord, after accepting Him as Savior, is to find someone to be an "accountability shepherd." That person should possess and display a consistent Christian walk. Their role would be to walk by your side to help you navigate your newfound friendship with Jesus.

Having an "accountability shepherd" to help you is like having an AA sponsor; someone you can call when you want to ask questions, someone you can trust with your thoughts, someone who will give good Christian advice and godly counsel, especially in times of need.

An "accountability shepherd" who helps you along your walk with Christ, isn't judgmental, but is knowledgeable in the Word and able to rebuke as needed in a godly manner. But most importantly, an "accountability shepherd" should have a proven track record of walking in the ways of Christ themselves.

My "accountability shepherd" Matt, helped me recognize my need for the Savior. He had a consistent walk with Christ. He listened to my questions no matter how naïve they may have seemed. He gave me anecdotes that addressed my questions or daily trials, and he provided advice on how to act as a Christian.

My "accountability shepherd" has witnessed the Holy Spirit overcome my life and break through the "tough guy" exterior. My "accountability shepherd" has watched me become overwhelmed by tears at the recognition of God's love. He has witnessed my struggles with sin every day and cheered me on through my toughest battles. He has seen me speak God's Word in fellowship groups and even through my personal testimony. He watches and witnesses God's work in me with reassuring encouragement.

Being accountable to another person helps a lot, especially when first becoming a Christian. For example, when I was newly saved, I had a hard time letting go of my habitual pattern of cursing. But I realized that I hardly ever would curse in my "accountability shepherd's" presence. I have curbed it a lot with conscious thought, but just his presence there alone reminds me of God's presence and makes me feel a little guilty, almost as if I'm failing them both when I slide backwards to my old ways. And it is through those times that I realize it is God—not any man, truly, that I am failing. It is God who is with me always whether I can see Him or not. My "accountability shepherd" keeps me mindful of that.

The battle between good and evil is a real battle being fought for our souls daily. The presence of my "accountability shepherd" along with fellow Christians around me, makes my faith even stronger. I am able to conquer my fleshly will with more spiritual muscle because I am being coached, encouraged and supported by my brothers-in-Christ.

If I wanted to be a carpenter, I wouldn't hang out with a plumber! If I want to be a strong Christian, I must surround myself with like-minded Christians. An "accountability shepherd" is someone I can learn from, to be a stronger Christian man.

THE WAY OF A FOOL IS RIGHT IN HIS OWN EYES, BUT HE WHO HEEDS COUNSEL IS WISE.

PROVERBS 12:15

DON'T BE AFRAID TO ASK QUESTIONS

SO, I SAY TO YOU, ASK, AND IT WILL BE GIVEN TO YOU; SEEK, AND YOU WILL FIND; KNOCK, AND IT WILL BE OPENED TO YOU.
LUKE 11:9

I have always been an inquisitive person wanting to know the who, what, when, and where of any given subject. I've never hesitated to ask questions. Some questions were on point, others fell short of the mark, and some even exposed how naïve I was on the particular subjects I inquired about. I would never have learned much if I were afraid to ask those questions in the first place though.

Upon becoming a Christian and embarking on this lifelong walk with Christ, I was filled with questions. At first, I was admittedly a bit apprehensive to ask lots of questions for fear of sounding skeptical of my newfound faith. I didn't want to sound like I was debating God's Word.

As time progressed, I prayed and asked God to give me understanding, knowledge, and answers through His Word. More times than not, the answer came with just the right Scripture, at just the right time.

I don't believe that there is such a thing as a stupid question. We always gain knowledge when we ask questions, and that in turn, can prepare us to assist someone else. I have learned that if we have accepted Christ as our Savior, then we can be assured that He will place people in our path (such as "accountability shepherds") who may be more knowledgeable in God's Word than we are, to help with those questions. We should take advantage of their knowledge not be afraid to ask, trusting that God too, has prepared these folks ahead of time to assist us.

In addition to the fellowship and wise counselors that God will provide around us, God makes it easy for His children to follow His Word through the powerful teaching of the Holy Spirit. Even so, we should remember that God's mysteries are still always revealed in His timing, as aligned with His plan.

Don't try to overthink every passage of the Bible. Concentrate on having His Holy Spirit fill you and empower you. He will guide you towards a decent, clean, and Spirit-led life. When you have a question, ask God! He will give you the answer through His Word, or through His daily workings in your life.

All you have to do is have faith in God and ask away.

> IF ANY OF YOU LACKS WISDOM, LET HIM ASK OF GOD, WHO GIVES TO ALL LIBERALLY AND WITHOUT REPROACH, AND IT WILL BE GIVEN TO HIM.
>
> JAMES 1:5

LOOK FOR GOD'S MESSAGE TO YOU

AND AFTER THE EARTHQUAKE A FIRE, BUT THE LORD WAS NOT IN THE FIRE; AND AFTER THE FIRE A STILL SMALL VOICE.

1 KINGS 19:19

God's messages come in many forms. He personalizes His message to His beloved children like an earthly father would to his own child. Each child of God is different and so His message may be heard and received uniquely as well.

As I already confessed, I had originally asked God to prove Himself to me by moving an ashtray. God knew that if He had done exactly that, that I would have brushed it off and rationalized it as the wind, or as the table moving instead. God knew me well enough to know that He had to move something that nobody else was capable of moving, in order to impress me. So, when God chose to undeniably move my hardened heart, instead of a mere ashtray - it was a very personal message to me that God not only heard me, but knew me intimately, and knew exactly what it would take to get my attention.

Please allow me to backtrack a bit to further shed light on this experience. Hours earlier, I had been to church and while sitting there with my now "accountability shepherd" Matt, I was unexplainably melancholy. I wasn't sad, I was just feeling lost and empty, like I needed something to fill my heart and lift my spirit.

As I listened to the preacher and observed him during his sermon, I saw a peace in him. I saw that same peace in Matt over the past few months we had spent together. And it was right then and there that I realized what it was I was missing. It was peace; it had eluded me my entire life. And I suddenly knew I wanted it for myself—but how would I get it? God was preparing my heart to hear Him by wanting the peace that only comes from Him.

When God moved my heart, as you read earlier, during the reading of the Word, His movement in me was so personal that the scene was incomprehensible to those around me. There I sat, a 330lb., bald headed, tattooed, notorious "tough guy" reduced to sobbing like a child in front of 20 other fellow inmates. My armor was shattered and I sat there exposed and vulnerable and for the first time, unashamed to do so, as I explained that I wanted what I saw in the others - that unexplainable, unfathomable peace!

Afterwards, I felt so clean, so free of my past that all I could do was smile. I know God had sent me a completely personalized message. I'm living proof that He wants to show Himself to us uniquely.

God didn't move the ashtray. He moved me!

THEN ALL THE MIDIANITES AND AMALEKITES, THE PEOPLE OF THE EAST, GATHERED TOGETHER; AND THEY CROSSED OVER AND ENCAMPED IN THE VALLEY OF JEZREEL. BUT THE SPIRIT OF THE LORD CAME UPON GIDEON; THEN HE BLEW THE TRUMPET, AND THE ABIEZRITES GATHERED BEHIND HIM. AND HE SENT MESSENGERS THROUGHOUT ALL MANASSEH, WHO ALSO GATHERED BEHIND HIM. HE ALSO SENT MESSENGERS TO ASHER, ZEBULUN, AND NAPHTALI; AND THEY CAME UP TO MEET THEM.

SO GIDEON SAID TO GOD, "IF YOU WILL SAVE ISRAEL BY MY HAND AS YOU HAVE SAID - LOOK, I SHALL PUT A FLEECE OF WOOL ON THE THRESHING FLOOR; IF THERE IS DEW ON THE FLEECE ONLY, AND IT IS DRY ON ALL THE GROUND, THEN I SHALL KNOW THAT YOU WILL SAVE ISRAEL BY MY HAND, AS

YOU HAVE SAID." AND IT WAS SO. WHEN HE ROSE EARLY THE NEXT MORNING AND SQUEEZED THE FLEECE TOGETHER, HE WRUNG THE DEW OUT OF THE FLEECE, A BOWLFUL OF WATER.

THEN GIDEON SAID TO GOD, "DO NOT BE ANGRY WITH ME, BUT LET ME SPEAK JUST ONCE MORE: LET ME TEST, I PRAY, JUST ONCE MORE WITH THE FLEECE; LET IT NOW BE DRY ONLY ON THE FLEECE, BUT ON ALL THE GROUND
LET THERE BE DEW."
AND GOD DID SO THAT NIGHT. IT WAS DRY ON THE FLEECE ONLY, BUT THERE WAS DEW ON ALL THE GROUND.
JUDGES 6:33-40

TELL OTHERS ABOUT YOUR EXPERIENCE

AND PAUL SAID, "I WOULD TO GOD THAT NOT ONLY YOU, BUT ALSO ALL WHO HEAR ME TODAY, MIGHT BECOME BOTH ALMOST AND ALTOGETHER SUCH AS I AM, EXCEPT FOR THESE CHAINS."
ACTS 26:29

Sharing your testimony is a very important part of your new Christian walk. By sharing your story, you are given a unique platform to tell others of your own personal experiences and what has brought you to know Christ as your personal Savior. There is no better way to glorify God than by displaying how your life has been changed by Him. Your testimony is unique to you alone, and sharing your struggles and your journey opens up the door for others to relate to you personally. Your testimony may help them find hope that if God changed your life so much, that theirs can be changed too.

My own personal story is long and sordid. I was once a professional criminal, womanizer, and epic party guy who had been in and out of prison for decades. God had tried to get my attention over the years, but unfortunately, I never recognized His attempts, nor would I have entertained them if I did.

It hadn't been until I was in my mid 40's, and unfortunately doing my fourth bid (prison sentence) that God made His presence known to me in an undoubtable, irrefutable, miraculous way. As I have explained in prior chapters, I made a statement in my foolish banter, challenging God for Him to prove Himself by moving an ashtray. And He responded. He moved that "ashtray" clear across the room.

I have since that day shared my experience with anyone willing to listen. God has given me a voice, along with the words to spread His Glory and merciful ways. I am humbled that God has chosen me to be used for His good to show people that by having faith and believing in Him, we all can be saved and share in the glory of Heaven. It doesn't matter where you are, what you have, or what you have done. Salvation is the free gift purchased through the brutal death and glorious resurrection of Jesus Christ.

By sharing my testimony and experience about God with others, I am hopeful that they will see how God has changed me for the better, brought me peace, and given me true joy in my life.

It is my prayer that my testimony and my life's spiritual consistency will give others a glimpse of God's power and bring all who hear it into God's waiting arms.

Testimony is a strong weapon. Share yours with others.

"FOR MY THOUGHTS ARE NOT YOUR THOUGHTS, NOR ARE YOUR WAYS MY WAYS," SAYS THE LORD. "FOR AS THE HEAVENS ARE HIGHER THAN THE EARTH, SO ARE MY WAYS HIGHER THAN YOUR WAYS, AND MY THOUGHTS THAN YOUR THOUGHTS."

ISAIAH 55: 8-9

AND THEY OVERCAME HIM BY THE BLOOD OF THE LAMB AND BY THE WORD OF THEIR TESTIMONY...

REVELATION 12:11

PRACTICE WHAT YOU PREACH

YOUR WORD HAVE I HIDDEN IN MY HEART, THAT I MIGHT NOT SIN AGAINST YOU.

PSALM 119:11

An old adage says, "Practice what you preach," and another similar one states, "Practice makes perfect." If we were to combine those two sayings, and acted upon them, we would have a life that possessed such strength, power, and wisdom, that it could change the world. "Practice what you preach, it could make you perfect." (In this case, "perfect" meaning a "complete" display of that which we are professing.) For Jesus, our actions are a direct display of our heart's commitment to Him (John 14:15).

How can I tell others how to walk as a Christian if I don't walk as one myself? People watch how you carry yourself at every step; especially if you are preaching the Word of God to them and sharing your testimony about what brought you to God.

I've been very blessed in my Christian walk thus far; it has been somewhat easy for me, mostly because I truly wanted change and peace in my life in a very big way. I realized from the start that I wanted and needed God in my life, but I was fearful of being a hypocrite or a failure in His eyes. I recognized the need for certain new "practices." I first voiced the changes I wanted and needed to make, to Jesus my "Heavenly Accountability Partner" and also to Matt, my "accountability shepherd" here on earth.

I started my practicing with nagging sins such as my foul mouth, my impure thoughts and my pride. I actively prayed and worked on being conscious of myself and my actions, and then worked my way up to regularly sharing my testimony and making it a point to read God's Word daily.

I heard someone say at a church service one night while still in prison, that by accepting Christ as our Savior, and by believing in God's Word, we are "ordained by God" to preach His word. I also believe that, you cannot preach what you do not practice yourself. It's like claiming to be a soccer pro when you have never actually kicked a ball.

By preaching what you practice, you set a very good example for those to whom you are speaking. Application of God's Word and His laws are paramount to practicing what we preach. If we choose to live our lives as Christians walking in the shadow of Christ, then we must preach God's Word, but more importantly, we must live by God's Word.

Practicing what you preach will make you more in touch with how to live God's truth and experience the blessings of His plan for you. God's Word is the truth. It is perfect in all of its majesty and if we read His Word and apply it to our lives, it will enable us to be examples of what He wants us to be, which in turn, allows us to preach His Word by our actions. We can be living Bibles because we are practicing it, living it, and applying it to our own lives. Make it a point to both preach and practice God's Word and perfect law.

BUT BE DOERS OF THE WORD, AND NOT HEARERS ONLY, DECEIVING YOURSELVES. FOR IF ANYONE IS A HEARER OF THE WORD AND NOT A DOER, HE IS LIKE A MAN OBSERVING HIS NATURAL FACE IN THE MIRROR; FOR HE OBSERVES HIMSELF, GOES AWAY, AND IMMEDIATELY FORGETS WHAT KIND OF MAN HE WAS. BUT HE WHO LOOKS INTO THE PERFECT LAW OF LIBERTY AND CONTINUES IN IT, AND IS NOT A FORGETFUL

HEARER BUT A DOER OF THE WORK, THIS ONE WILL BE BLESSED

IN WHAT HE DOES.

JAMES 1:22-25

THE POWER OF OUR WORDS AND DEEDS

AND WHATEVER YOU DO IN WORD OR DEED, DO ALL IN THE NAME OF THE LORD JESUS, GIVING THANKS TO GOD THE FATHER THROUGH HIM.
COLOSSIANS 3:17

Words are one of the most powerful tools we have in our lives. They can be used to inflict great harm or to show love and affection. Words can lift a person up; or discourage them and keep them down. That is precisely why it is very important that we choose our words very carefully in life and consciously review how we communicate with others.

As Christians we should aim to inspire with our words; edifying, loving, and lifting one another. As God's Word to us, the Bible has great meaning and it is by His Word that we should learn how to model our own words.

Deeds are the acts we perform. I have always wanted to be remembered for the good deeds I have done instead of the bad. I heard someone say once, "You're only as good as your last good deed." If that is true, I want to make all of my last deeds reflect God's glory. We must put God first, always trying through the power of the Holy Spirit to do the good work He's created, and prepared for us to do.

As stated earlier, my bad language was one of the things I struggled with most when I first became a Christian. I used to curse a lot; never realizing just how unattractive those foul words made me look to others. Now I realize, as I listen to others speak, how foul language can make someone sound unintelligent and ignorant. Foul language can and will make you unattractive to those around you; and it can embarrass and shame the people you are with, especially in public. As a Christian, we must learn to replace those foul and dirty words with other words that are more glorifying to God and honoring to others, and ourselves.

With God's help and through prayer, He will strengthen our spirits and make it so much easier for us to think consciously about our conduct and speech.

We should adopt the awareness of a child, recognizing that we are continuously being watched by a loving parent. When we think of God and His watchful eye over us, we can become more conscious of our words and deeds. We must be the best examples we can be as Christians, because our words and deeds become a witness to the power of Christ. As my "accountability shepherd" Matt said in his book, we may be the only Bible someone reads![1]

We are responsible for our own words and deeds and the impact they may have on others, so be conscious of your words, deeds, and language. It makes our Christian walk more appealing to others.

LET US HEAR THE CONCLUSION OF THE WHOLE MATTER: FEAR GOD AND KEEP HIS COMMANDMENTS, FOR THIS IS MAN'S ALL. FOR GOD WILL BRING EVERY WORK INTO JUDGMENT, INCLUDING EVERY SECRET THING, WHETHER GOOD OR EVIL.

ECCLESIASTES 12:13-14

---

[1] *You May B the Only Bible Somebody Reads: R U Legible,* Matthew Maher 55:11 Publishing, Philadelphia, PA.

TALK TO GOD WHEN YOU WANT TO

SEEK THE LORD WHILE HE MAY BE FOUND, CALL UPON HIM WHILE HE IS NEAR.

ISAIAH 55:6

Many children pray at night on bended knee by their bed sides. Some people pray on the holidays and others open their day with prayer. What I've learned through my "accountability shepherd" Matt, is that formal solemn prayer is great, but it doesn't have to take on a routine or formality in order for it to reach God. As believers, we have the privilege to talk to God as easily as we can any earthly person. And He is always available for us. All we have to do is verbalize our thoughts or think our conversation in our mind and hearts.

God is listening, it's that simple, go ahead and try it.

I have found this constant communication with God to be extremely soothing and very helpful in keeping my thoughts in line with my Christian walk. Speaking with God throughout my day also keeps my foul mouth in check along with my thoughts and temperament.

God has the answers to even our hardest questions. He has the advice we need and the wisdom we crave. By speaking with God as a Father, Friend, Mentor, and Guide we can be sure to get truthful answers to our most heartfelt questions.

Even when we don't perceive the answer in the right way, God never fails with an answer; nor does He fail in His plan. So, take the time to talk with God, He is here for us, and He is a great listener.

I SOUGHT THE LORD, AND HE HEARD ME, AND DELIVERED ME FROM ALL MY FEARS.

PSALM 34:4

'CALL TO ME, AND I WILL ANSWER YOU, AND SHOW YOU GREAT AND MIGHTY THINGS, WHICH YOU DO NOT KNOW.'

JEREMIAH 33:3

LIVE A GOOD CLEAN LIFE

DELIGHT YOURSELF ALSO IN THE LORD, AND HE SHALL GIVE YOU THE DESIRES OF YOUR HEART.
PSALM 37:4

You've likely heard the old saying "Cleanliness is next to Godliness!" While this phrase is not actually in the Bible, much of the instruction of the Bible directs us toward clean, holy living. I'm not just talking hygiene here. I'm speaking about the cleanliness of the soul, the mind, and the body.

As Christians, we must aim to keep our souls clean. While Jesus' blood has forever washed us from the eternal penalty of sin, we should be active to still apply daily the soap of the soul - God's Word - to our minds, hearts and actions to continue in our pursuit of holy, clean living.

It is important to God that we take care of our body - His temple - as it holds the mind, heart and our eternal soul which follows Christ the Savior into everlasting life beyond this one. Our bodies, as His Temple, should be swept clean of any debris or clutter that would keep us from being able to be healthy, strong, focused, and fit.

God wants His army strong. We must stay healthy by eating and exercising correctly. What we put in our bodies is critical for how effectively they will endure. Food and drink are good as long they are not abused.

Our minds must stay focused on God and Jesus; thinking as God would want us to think and trying to emulate Jesus' ways. We must keep our minds clean of impure thoughts, clean of negativity, and focused on God and His direction for our Christian lives.

THEREFORE, HAVING THESE PROMISES, BELOVED, LET US CLEANSE OURSELVES FROM ALL FILTHINESS OF THE FLESH AND SPIRIT, PERFECTING HOLINESS IN THE FEAR OF GOD.

2 CORINTHIANS 7:1

PRAISE GOD ALWAYS – GOOD OR BAD

REJOICE IN THE LORD ALWAYS. AGAIN, I WILL SAY, REJOICE!
PHILIPPIANS 4:4

It's easy to praise God when things are going great; it's easy to thank Him for prosperity. But what I've come to learn is that God's will and plan is preordained and even through bad times in our lives, He knows the beginning, the end, and the purpose to it all. In Romans 8:28, the Bible reassures us that He works all things to the good of those who love Him.

It's hard to be grateful for a trial or give praise for tribulation. Have any of us ever said thank you to a parent for a spanking or a punishment? I can't ever remember being punished and saying, "Thanks Dad, I needed that, I now see the error of my ways." No, instead I felt wronged and resentful toward the parents that were only trying to correct behavior that they realized held the weight of serious consequences later in life – such as prison, or death.

Now, thanks be to God, with children of my own, (Samantha, Sasha, and Brittany) I see how foolish I was, not heeding my own parent's instruction.

I've come to find out that God is our Heavenly Father and we would be wise to heed His all-knowing instruction. He wants us, His earthly children, to be wise and understand that when He allows trials and tribulations into our lives, it is because He has plans to use them for good.

We need to understand that those trials and tribulations are sometimes the exact thing we need in our lives in order to learn and grow as we conform to the image of Jesus.

Praise God for the tests He places in our lives! Praise God for taking the time to discipline and correct us as necessary when we are going left as we need to go right! Praise God for His trials and tribulations because we can consider it all joy (James 1:2) as He works in our lives through all things!

It's easy to thank God when things are good. However, thanks are always in order because we serve a righteous God, and for that alone, He deserves all of our praise and gratitude. Praising God for tests, trials, and tribulations may come a little harder, but once we understand the value of the lesson, we must thank God for taking the time to discipline and train us; as only a caring Father would do for His children.

Praise God for *all* He does in your life, "good" or "bad" it is *all* a part of His Glorious plan for our lives.

THOUGH THE FIG TREE MAY NOT BLOSSOM, NOR FRUIT BE ON THE VINES; THOUGH THE LABOR OF THE OLIVE MAY FAIL, AND THE FIELDS YIELD NO FOOD; THOUGH THE FLOCK MAY BE CUT OFF FROM THE FOLD, AND THERE BE NO HERD IN THE STALLS - YET I WILL REJOICE IN THE LORD, I WILL JOY IN THE GOD OF MY SALVATION.

HABAKKUK 3:17-18

MY BRETHREN, COUNT IT ALL JOY WHEN YOU FALL INTO VARIOUS TRIALS, KNOWING THAT THE TESTING OF YOUR FAITH PRODUCES PATIENCE.

JAMES 1:2-3

YOU CAN LEAD 'EM TO WATER (GOD'S WORD) BUT YOU CAN'T MAKE 'EM A CHRISTIAN

GO THEREFORE AND MAKE DISCIPLES OF ALL THE NATIONS, BAPTIZING THEM IN THE NAME OF THE FATHER AND OF THE SON AND OF THE HOLY SPIRIT...

MATTHEW 28:19

My "accountability shepherd" Matt and I hit it off from the start. It was easy for him to preach God's Word to me because I was open to change; realizing that change could only come through having God in my life and Jesus as my Savior.

As Christians, with Jesus in our hearts, it seems only natural that we should want to let others know about the saving grace and cleansing power of His shed blood for our sins and how we can have eternal life in a glorious beautiful Heaven, alongside of Him.

Being a Christian is like eating in the finest restaurant and wanting everyone you know and love to have the same delightful experience. We may put great effort into telling others of this incredible destination, but no matter how hard we try, we can't make anyone go and eat there. For some, the cuisine or flavor may not interest them. For others, it may seem like too far to travel, or that the prices are too high. Such is the case with our efforts to spread the Gospel message.

Matt and I spent countless hours in prison trying to reach as many people as we could. Some listened and applied what we taught them; others listened from a distance. Some just wanted to debate, while others refused to hear a word.

At first, I was offended and wanted to beat Jesus into their lives, but fortunately for them Matt explained how that just isn't the Christian way. I've had to accept the fact that we can preach the Word of God and give testimony and some will drink; while others won't yet be thirsty.

Matt and I tried to make our testimony and the lessons interesting to those we spoke with, but some just weren't ready to hear. I realize that it took God 45 years to move my "ashtray," and His timing in it, was perfect. I am learning to realize His timing is perfect with others as well.

All we can do is continue to spread God's message and hope that by leading people to the water – the living water, Jesus Christ through God's Word - that they will drink. If not, we must understand that it may not be God's plan for that person's life at that exact moment, no matter how "perfect" *we* think the timing is.

Making believers is God's business through the power of the Holy Spirit. We are only the water bearers. So, lead as many as you can to the water of God's Word and if they are thirsty, then God-willing, they will drink.

...AND FOR ME, THAT UTTERANCE MAY BE GIVEN TO ME, THAT I MAY OPEN MY MOUTH BOLDLY TO MAKE KNOWN THE MYSTERY OF THE GOSPEL, FOR WHICH I AM AN AMBASSADOR IN CHAINS; THAT IN IT I MAY SPEAK BOLDLY, AS I OUGHT TO SPEAK.
EPHESIANS 6:19-20

FOR WE ARE HIS WORKMANSHIP, CREATED IN CHRIST JESUS FOR GOOD WORKS, WHICH GOD PREPARED BEFOREHAND THAT

WE SHOULD WALK IN THEM.

EPHESIANS 2:10

"BUT THE HELPER, THE HOLY SPIRIT, WHOM THE FATHER WILL SEND IN MY NAME, HE WILL TEACH YOU ALL THINGS, AND BRING TO YOUR REMEMBRANCE ALL THINGS THAT I SAID TO YOU."

JOHN 14:26

SIN IS SIN – BIG OR SMALL

...FOR ALL HAVE SINNED AND FALL SHORT
OF THE GLORY OF GOD.
ROMANS 3:23

I think the idea of trying not sin on a huge scale prevents some people from keeping "smaller" sins in check. For me, I am trying to keep the "smaller" sins in check because I realize that they are like an open gateway to the "bigger sins."

Through the reading of God's Word though, I realize that a sin is a sin; "big" or "small." There is no difference to God, as all sin separates us from Him. All of our sin, "big" or "small" comes with the same consequence - which according to Romans 6:23, is death.

As I wrote most of this devotional in prison, I realized then, that the temptations I was regularly exposed to were minimal, compared to that which I would face being released to the street once more. For me, this may have just been the reason why God chose to turn my heart towards Him then. He knew the temptations on the street may have kept me from knowing or learning about Him without the worldly distractions.

God has chosen to break through the veil I once had covering my eyes. He has shown me that He is listening to me and wants me to be with Him and His Son, Jesus Christ in Heaven. I'm grateful to have become more aware of that which I previously would have only considered "small" sins that offend my God.

I've come to understand that the sins that most of us consider "small" are the sins that slip in daily and corrupt us unwittingly because we feel they are insignificant. But sin of any size is transgression against God. Cursing, lying, using the Lord's name in vain, cheating, pride, envy, gluttony, jealously, impure thoughts, etc... these are the sins we most overlook while we're busy trying not to commit the "big" sins like killing, robbing, adultery, or worse. All of these sins denounce God and the glory due to Him.

I feel that if we, as Christians, can be watchful of these "small" sins we can become much closer to God and our examples may inspire the same in others, in the process.

I make it a habit to ask the Holy Spirit to help me to be mindful of all my sins—especially the "small" ones that creep in daily. I have been striving to have days where I do not have to ask God for His forgiveness. I want to have a day where all I do is praise God and enjoy the power and presence of His Holy Spirit leading my life.

"YOU HAVE HEARD THAT IT WAS SAID TO THOSE OF OLD, 'YOU SHALL NOT MURDER, AND WHOEVER MURDERS WILL BE IN DANGER OF THE JUDGMENT.' BUT I SAY TO YOU THAT WHOEVER IS ANGRY WITH HIS BROTHER WITHOUT A CAUSE SHALL BE IN DANGER OF THE JUDGMENT. AND WHOEVER SAYS TO HIS BROTHER, 'RACA!' SHALL BE IN DANGER OF THE COUNCIL. BUT WHOEVER SAYS, 'YOU FOOL!' SHALL BE IN DANGER OF HELL FIRE."

MATTHEW 5:21-22

"YOU HAVE HEARD THAT IT WAS SAID TO THOSE OF OLD, 'YOU SHALL NOT COMMIT ADULTERY.' BUT I SAY TO YOU THAT WHOEVER LOOKS AT A WOMAN TO LUST FOR HER HAS ALREADY COMMITTED ADULTERY WITH HER IN HIS HEART."

MATTHEW 5:27-28

FOR THE WAGES OF SIN IS DEATH, BUT THE GIFT OF GOD IS ETERNAL LIFE IN CHRIST JESUS OUR LORD.

ROMANS 6:23

SUBMIT TO GOD

BUT HE GIVES MORE GRACE. THEREFORE, HE SAYS: "GOD RESISTS THE PROUD, BUT GIVES GRACE TO THE HUMBLE." THEREFORE, SUBMIT TO GOD. RESIST THE DEVIL AND HE WILL FLEE FROM YOU.

JAMES 4:6-7

One definition of submit states: To yield to another; to present for consideration—to surrender; obey. When I think of Christian submission, I think of us willingly falling backwards - knowing that God is already there with the plan to catch us and provide for our well-being. It is the realization that He is waiting with open arms, waiting for us to let go, to submit to His will, His plan, His love, His mercy, His forgiveness, and His understanding. He wants to see that we trust Him to do what He promises.

For me, submitting to God also means being able to recognize that I simply can't do "it" alone. It's the realization that I need to submit to God's plan and let Him take over, in order to help me come through my sorrows, trials and tribulations.

We can yield to God, give God the right of way, let Him take over, lay "it" all at His feet and allow Him to work in us and with us. We can present ourselves for consideration, place *ourselves* at God's feet, bent down on our knees willing to proceed and participate with His will to do as He sees fit.

In order to surrender fully in this way, I've prayed prayers such as this: "I surrender to You, Father God, use me as You see fit." Let God know you're not going to fight Him any longer, that you surrender to His will and His glory in your life.

Obey God, His Word and His law. Obey the ten commandments. Let God's will be done in you and around you always. Obey God in all circumstances to the best of your ability and understanding. Submit your will to God and He will bring you to heights you have never imagined.

THE SACRIFICES OF GOD ARE A BROKEN SPIRIT, A BROKEN AND A CONTRITE HEART - THESE, O GOD, YOU WILL NOT DESPISE.

PSALM 51:17

THOUGH THE LORD IS ON HIGH, YET HE REGARDS THE LOWLY; BUT THE PROUD HE KNOWS FROM AFAR.

PSALM 138:6

IN LOVE

"TEACHER, WHICH IS THE GREAT COMMANDMENT IN THE LAW?" JESUS SAID TO HIM, "'YOU SHALL LOVE THE LORD YOUR GOD WITH ALL YOUR HEART, WITH ALL YOUR SOUL, AND WITH ALL YOUR MIND.' THIS IS THE FIRST AND GREAT COMMANDMENT. AND THE SECOND IS LIKE IT: 'YOU SHALL LOVE YOUR NEIGHBOR AS YOURSELF.'"

MATTHEW 22:36-39

Being in love with Jesus should be like being in a beautiful relationship where you want nothing more than to please your mate. Anyone who has ever been in love knows the newness of that feeling and the excitement that accompanies it. That is how we should act when we find our new relationship with God.

If we can desire to please an earthly mate in love, then we should strive to have an even deeper love for our Savior who loves us to even the depths of our soul.

We should keep the freshness of our relationship with Christ new and birthed daily. We need to keep our hearts focused on love for God and not allow our relationship with Christ to become stale or routine. God's Word is a gift we can receive daily. His love is a blessing we need to recognize daily. God loves us with a fresh new love every day; we should do the same toward Him.

I don't think we can honestly say we know the true meaning of love in its entirety until we have suffered the loss of, or have been separated from it.

God knew that to verbalize love wasn't enough for us to believe He loved us. His heavenly and spiritually divine love can hardly be explained with mere words, but His blood speaks volumes.

If I asked you whether you loved me and you said, "Yes, I love you John," and I said "Well, prove it by killing the person you love most," would you?

Abraham was so in love with God that he was willing to kill his only son to prove to God that he was obedient to Him and loved and trusted Him. God loved us so much, that He did what He Himself asked of

Abraham. He sacrificed His only Son, shed His blood, and made Him become the sacrifice for our sin so we might be washed clean not just by Christ's blood, but by God's love for us.

My love for God spoken, thought of, and felt, must be backed by deeds and action as His was, and by reading His Word. This is how I can show God that I love Him and always will. How, in this day, can you love and enjoy being in love with the One who saved you?

"THE LORD HAS APPEARED OF OLD TO ME, SAYING: "YES, I HAVE LOVED YOU WITH AN EVERLASTING LOVE; THEREFORE, WITH LOVINGKINDNESS I HAVE DRAWN YOU."
JEREMIAH 31:3

AND NOW ABIDE FAITH, HOPE, AND LOVE, THESE THREE; BUT THE GREATEST OF THESE IS LOVE.
1 CORINTHIANS 13:13

TO CONSOLE THOSE WHO MOURN IN ZION, TO GIVE THEM BEAUTY FOR ASHES, THE OIL OF JOY FOR MOURNING, THE GARMENT OF PRAISE FOR THE SPIRIT OF HEAVINESS; THAT THEY MAY BE CALLED TREES OF RIGHTEOUSNESS, THE PLANTING OF THE LORD, THAT HE MAY BE GLORIFIED.
ISAIAH 61:3

GOD SENSE

FOR OF HIM AND THROUGH HIM AND TO HIM ARE ALL THINGS, TO WHOM BE GLORY FOREVER. AMEN.
ROMANS 11:36

Knowing about God and "knowing God" are two different things. Most people know about God, have heard about God, or seen the name of Jesus printed on a bumper sticker or t-shirt. Many people wear crosses as jewelry around their neck signifying a reference to God. But what does it really mean to know God?

Knowing and finding God, (not that He is lost), consists of the realization that you are a sinner in need of a Savior. It's responding to His call to enter into a personal relationship with Him. It's asking Him to come into your life, take over your heart, infuse your soul, and retrain your brain to have communion with Him. This is all done through the reading of His Word, which is where we need to go to learn about His character and His ways. The Bible is an instruction book that guides our lives in all areas. The Word is alive and has relevance for all time.

How easy is it to look around and experience God with all five of our senses? His plan and design are in the smallest and largest of all created things. In order for us to enjoy them, all we have to do is open our eyes along with our hearts, to God and His Son.

Oh, how much I missed all of these years walking blindly with my eyes wide open. I thought my sight was far superior in darkness; and now in light, I see I was totally blind. I had scales covering all my senses rendering them crippled and useless. When I asked Christ to save me, the scales fell off. Now I see with new eyes, speak with a new tongue, and hear with godly openness. The newness confounds me and excites my senses. It causes me to praise Him and all of His creation.

With my new eyes I see a beauty that surrounds me daily because of God—no matter where I am. I see trees sway and dance along with the grasses in the fields, all to the music of a soft gentle breeze. My eyes now see beautiful flowers that blossom as the seasons change; and the brilliance of a pure white snow covering high peaks.

With a new heart, I understand how perfect God's plan was to create us in His image, how every man, woman, and child are His children and He, our Father.

God's plan allows us to hear His word and enjoy all of the beautiful sounds around us which shows His hand at work. With new ears, I hear how sweet God's Word is to listen to, how wise, knowledgeable and prudent those words are to hear. I now hear how joyful a child's laughter sounds floating through the air, and the majesty of a lion's roar. I hear differently, the sound of rain hitting the streets and the leaves rustling in the wind. I can now listen to the soft whisper of a bee's buzz or the fluttering of a humming bird's wings.

I now appreciate the fragrant delights of His creation that float through the air occasionally such as the aroma of a rose and the smell of the salty sea on a gentle wind. I have a renewed sense of the smell of the sweetness in the soil as a tomato plant grows in the dark dirt and the earthy fragrance when a late-autumn leaf is rubbed. There is a difference to the smell of fresh rain while it falls cleansing the earth like a global shower, and the new scent early in the morning on a perfect summer day.

How wondrous is God's plan to allow us the pleasure of recognizing His creation in new ways, even while our eyes are closed?

All He asks for us to do is to worship Him and accept His Son Jesus Christ as our personal Savior and we will be able to appreciate His beauty beyond our wildest imagination. Earthly things compare not at all to the Heavenly bounty in store for us when we as Christians, reach our place, by our Heavenly Father's side.

He is knocking on the door just waiting for you to answer. Allow Him to reawaken your senses. Experience God, for He is real. I know this for I have experienced Him. God is all around you.

So, ask God to open your eyes to His word and His testimony through others. Ask Him to open your eyes to the miracles He performs daily in the lives of those around you and to allow the beauty of His green earth to infiltrate your senses. That is how we develop our "God sense;" our knowledge of Him!

With renewed sight, we can realize that we are living wonders on earth because of God's plan and love. We live, so let us praise Him and give thanks for our lives and the blood of His Son, whom we have to be our Savior.

Praise the Lord! Praise the Lord from the heavens; Praise Him in the heights! Praise Him, all His angels; Praise Him, all His hosts! Praise Him, sun and moon; Praise Him, all you stars of light! Praise Him, you heavens of heavens, And you waters above the heavens! Let them praise the name of the Lord, For He commanded and they were created. He also established them forever and ever; He made a decree which shall not pass away. Praise the Lord from the earth, You great sea creatures and all the depths; Fire and hail, snow and clouds; Stormy wind, fulfilling His word; Mountains and all hills; Fruitful trees and all cedars; Beasts and all cattle; Creeping things and flying fowl; Kings of the earth and all peoples; Princes and all judges of the earth; Both young men and maidens; Old men and children. Let them praise the name of the Lord, For His name alone is exalted; His glory is above the earth and heaven. And He has exalted the horn of His people, The praise of all His saints - Of the children of Israel, A people near to Him. Praise the Lord!

Psalm 148

YOUR ASHTRAY CAN BE MOVED TOO!

"IF A SON ASKS FOR BREAD FROM ANY FATHER AMONG YOU, WILL HE GIVE HIM A STONE? OR IF HE ASKS FOR A FISH, WILL HE GIVE HIM A SERPENT INSTEAD OF A FISH? OR IF HE ASKS FOR AN EGG, WILL HE OFFER HIM A SCORPION? IF YOU THEN, BEING EVIL, KNOW HOW TO GIVE GOOD GIFTS TO YOUR CHILDREN, HOW MUCH MORE WILL YOUR HEAVENLY FATHER GIVE THE HOLY SPIRIT TO THOSE WHO ASK HIM!"

LUKE 11:11-13

It is my hope in this devotional that you have heard that God is a good God, who wants us to be near to Him. He desires for us to enjoy His purpose and plan. As I have already experienced for myself, it is as simple as asking Jesus, The Christ, to come into your life. He will move your "ashtray" as He moved mine.

At times, faith is hard and that is because faith is walking without seeing. It's trusting that God will guide your steps before you see the step. But as you proceed in faith, God will show you through His words, actions, and miracles how to keep it strong. When you lean on Him, He will put your feet on the right path.

God is not beholden to time. He works in a timeless economy. He will do His deeds when and where He sees fit to do them. Don't be discouraged, if you pray for a thing today expecting it to come to pass tomorrow and it doesn't. If God hasn't answered your prayer yet, or when or how you want it done, have the faith to know His plan is still good and perfect. He is not Santa Claus, or an ATM machine. He has paid our debt by dying on a cross and giving us the free gift of eternal life through salvation in His Son Jesus Christ.

God moves "ashtrays" in His own time, in His own personal way. He knows us each individually. It's not a one-stop salvation formula that's recognizable to all. He sees us uniquely and knows what we need to grow our faith in Him. He desires that we fellowship with Him and we do that by opening His Word, praying (talking to Him), and spending time with other believers. As your faith grows, He will give you eyes to see well beyond your personal "ashtray" challenge. He will move you and guide your steps daily.

All this happens through a simple request to God to change your life. Just ask! In the Bible, David says we can "taste and see" that the Lord is good (Psalm 34:8). Watch how He brings you into His fold, cares for, and loves you as His precious child. I never thought I would ever have God in my life. I wasn't even aware I was looking for Him to begin with. But He looked into my heart and He knew what I needed before I ever did. And once I asked, He answered. When I needed Him to reveal Himself to me—He did! He was always there just waiting for me to hear Him knocking on the door of my heart. His grace fell upon me without judgment or condemnation for who I was in my past. He is all loving, all forgiving. I can't help but declare that His mercy is great, His kindness never fails, and He is ever-faithful.

God moved my "ashtray" further across any table imaginable. Why? Because my heart hungered for proof and He sees deeply into our heart. I wanted to pledge my faith in Him. I desired to have a relationship of love and belief in Him. He was the One to put that desire in me. He took me up on my request and challenged me to not be unbelieving any longer!

I cannot and will not deny, what I felt and saw with my own eyes. What I know has changed in my heart and spirit can only be attributed to His supernatural touch. What I asked for - God has now given me - a pervading peace that passes all my natural understanding. And He continues to provide so much more for me in my life. I pray that you too, will invite and personally experience God moving your own "ashtray."

"BUT YOU SHALL RECEIVE POWER WHEN THE HOLY SPIRIT HAS COME UPON YOU; AND YOU SHALL BE WITNESSES TO ME IN JERUSALEM, AND IN ALL JUDEA AND SAMARIA, AND TO THE END OF THE EARTH."
ACTS 1:8

THEN PETER SAID TO THEM, "REPENT, AND LET EVERY ONE OF YOU BE BAPTIZED IN THE NAME OF JESUS CHRIST FOR THE REMISSION OF SINS; AND YOU SHALL RECEIVE THE GIFT OF THE HOLY SPIRIT."
ACTS 2:38

NOW HOPE DOES NOT DISAPPOINT, BECAUSE THE LOVE OF GOD HAS BEEN POURED OUT IN OUR HEARTS BY THE HOLY SPIRIT WHO WAS GIVEN TO US.
ROMANS 5:5

CALL TO ME, AND I WILL ANSWER YOU, AND SHOW YOU GREAT AND MIGHT THINGS, WHICH YOU DO NOT KNOW.
JEREMIAH 33:3

ABOUT THE AUTHOR:

John Paladino grew up on the streets of northern New Jersey. He is one of two kids from an Italian family. He began breaking the law at age 10; which eventually led to a life of crime into young adulthood and resulted in him spending the next 20 years in and out of prison. John has been called many things in his life, from hoodlum to tough guy, and more serious monikers like gangster and murderer--all of which are buried with his past since he encountered the Lord in his last stint of prison. Presently, by God's grace alone, "Little John" is now called Christian. For any inquiries about John, please go to www.truthovertrend.com/contact and drop us a message.

IF YOU ENJOYED THIS BOOK, WILL YOU CONSIDER SHARING THE INFLUENCE WITH OTHERS?

- Share or mention the book on your social media platforms.
- Recommend this book to those in your small group, book club, Bible study, workplace, and classes.
- Pick up a copy for someone you know who would be spiritually challenged and biblically charged by this message.
- Write a book review on amazon.com, bn.com, goodreads.com, or cbd.com

Made in the
USA
Middletown, DE